# Life Cycle of a

# Kangaroo

Angela Royston



Heinemann Interactive Library
Des Plaines, Illinois

Published by Heinemann Interactive Library,
an imprint of Reed Educational & Professional Publishing,
1350 East Touhy Avenue, Suite 240 West
Des Plaines, IL 60018



Designed by Celia Floyd
Illustrations by Alan Fraser
Printed In Hong Kong by South China Printing Co. (1988) Ltd.

02 01 00 99 98
10 9 8 7 6 5 4 3 2 1

**Library of Congress Cataloging-in-Publication Data**

Royston, Angela.
Life cycle of a kangaroo / by Angela Royston.
p. cm.
Includes index.
Summary: An introduction to the life cycle of a kangaroo from its first few months in its mother's pouch until it is four years old.
ISBN 1-57572-615-7 (lib. bdg.)
1. Kangaroos--Life cycles--Juvenile literature. [1. Kangaroos.]
I. Title.
QL737.M35R69 1998
599.2'22--dc21
97-39696
CIP
AC

**Acknowledgements**
The Publisher would like to thank the following for permission to reproduce photographs:
Bruce Coleman & DW Frith p4; Bruce Coleman & J Bartlett p24;
Bruce Coleman/Hans Reinhard p13; Bruce Coleman/John Canalosi p5, 10;
Nature Focus/A Young p6; NHPA/A N T p15; NHPA/Dave Watts p20, 21;
NHPA/Karl Switak p9; NHPA/Ken Griffiths pp18, 26/27; NHPA/Norbert Wu p25;
OSF/Alan Root p7; OSF/David B Fleetham p17; OSF/Kathie Atkinson pp11, 16;
OSF/Peter O'Toole p12; OSF/Stanley Breeden p22; OSF/Tom McHugh p19; Survival Anglia/D & J Bartlett p8, 14, 23.

Cover photograph: Art Wolfe/Tony Stone Images

# Contents

# Meet the Kangaroos

There are 50 different kinds of kangaroo. The one in this picture lives up in trees. Another kind is as small as a rat. They all live in Australia.

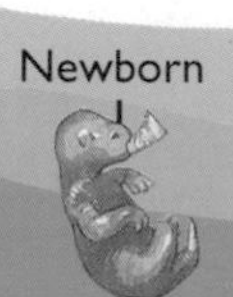

7 months

The kangaroo in this book is a Grey kangaroo.

Every kangaroo spends the first few months of its life in its mother's **pouch**.

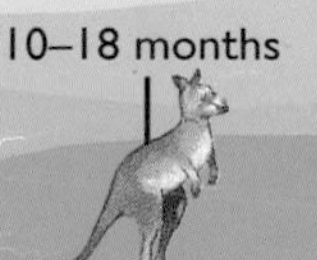

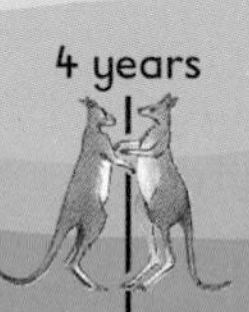

# Newborn

A baby kangaroo is called a **joey**. Just before the joey is born, its mother licks the inside of her **pouch** to make it ready for the joey.

Newborn

5 months

7 months

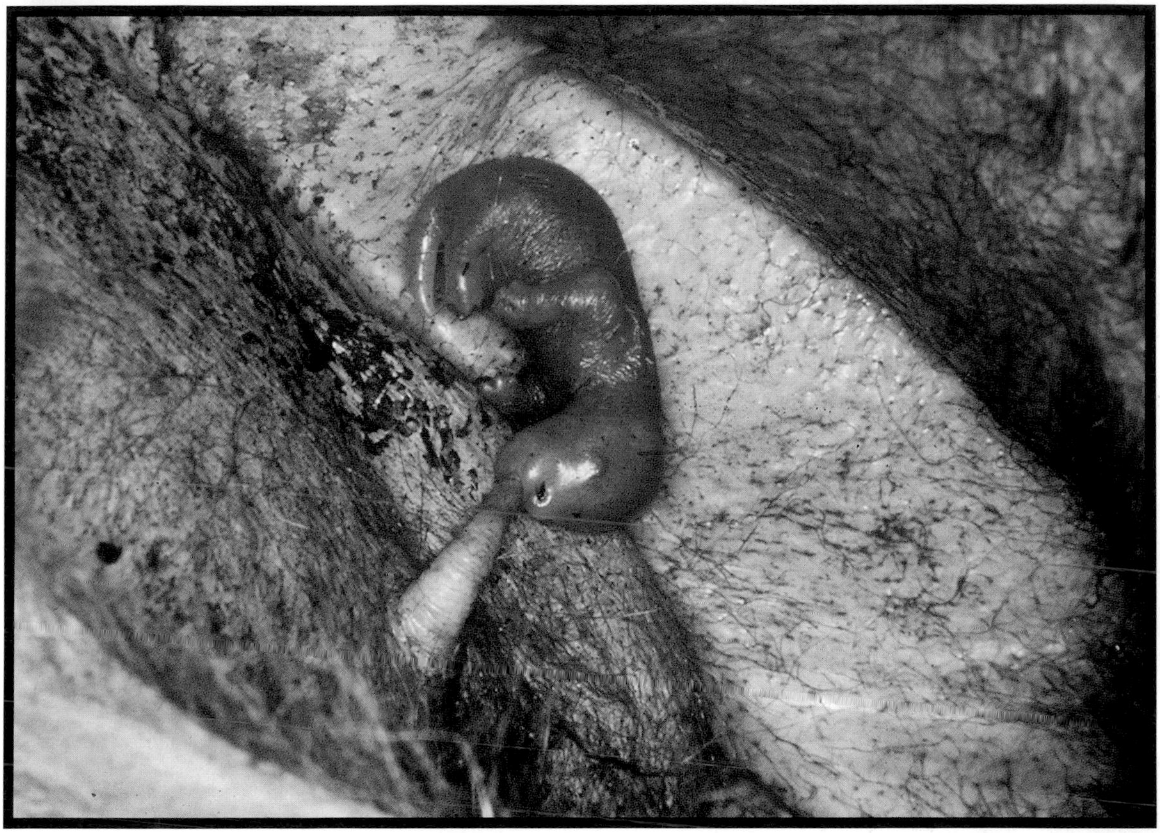

The newborn joey is tiny. It crawls through its mother’s fur and into her pouch. There it finds a **teat** and holds on tight with its mouth.

10–18 months

2 years

4 years

# Joey 5 to 6 months

The **joey** drinks milk from his mother and grows bigger. He can poke his head out of the **pouch** and look around.

The joey is safe inside the pouch. While his mother feeds, he eats some grass. When he is old enough his mother will tip him out of the pouch!

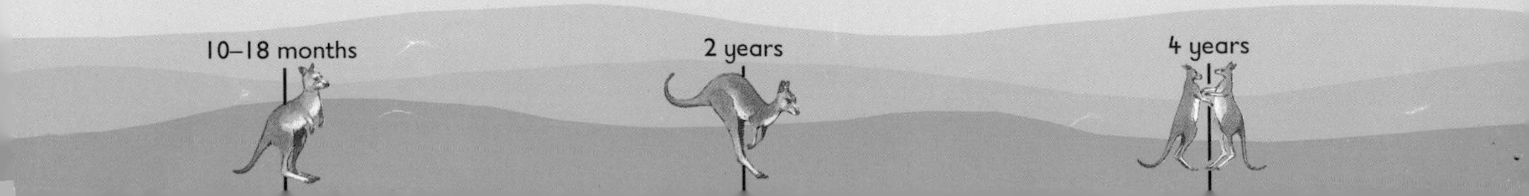

10–18 months

2 years

4 years

# 6 to 8 months

At first the **joey** is scared. But soon he is bouncing around. He can also **box** and play with his mother.

When he is thirsty, he dips his head into her **pouch** for a drink of milk. When he is tired, he climbs back in.

10–18 months

2 years

4 years

# 8 months

While the **joey** plays, his mother looks out for danger. Eagles likes to eat joeys and this one may attack.

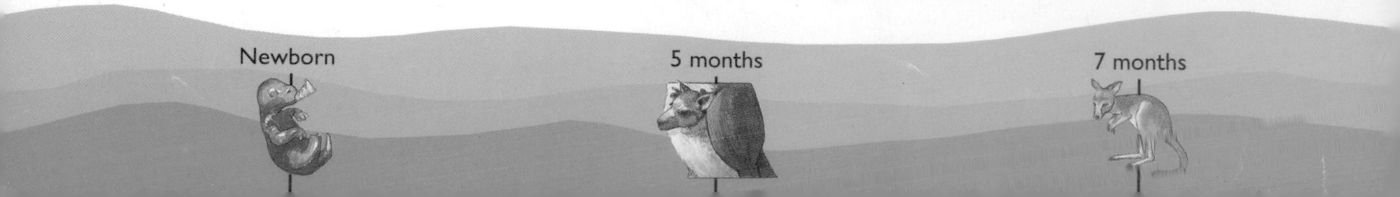

Newborn

5 months

7 months

His mother calls a warning to the joey and he dives head-first into her **pouch** for safety. He turns around inside the pouch.

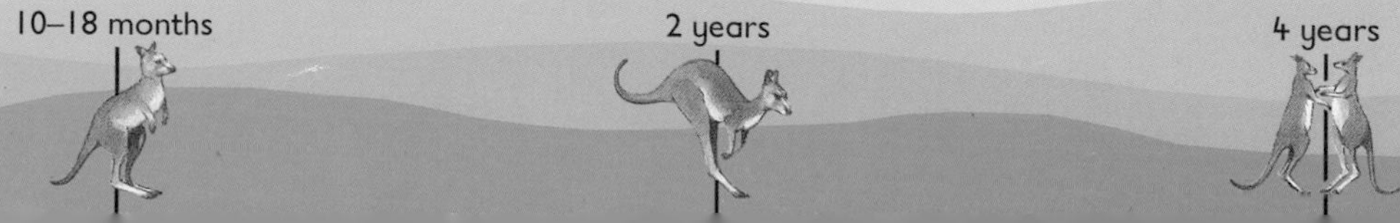

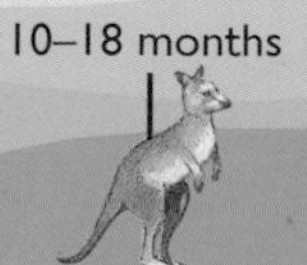

# 10 to 18 months

The **joey** is too big to get into the **pouch** now. He plays with the other joeys, but he still drinks his mother's milk.



Newborn

5 months

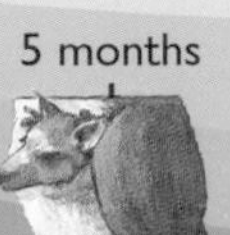

7 months

The joey stays very close to his mother. When she bounds away, he hurries after her!

10–18 months

2 years

4 years

# 18 months to 2 years

The kangaroos and **joeys** stay together in a big group. They feed on grass and leaves.

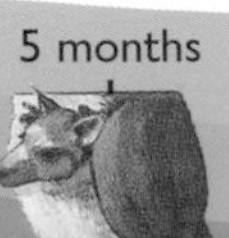

They feed early in the morning or late at night. During the heat of the day, they rest in the shade of the trees.

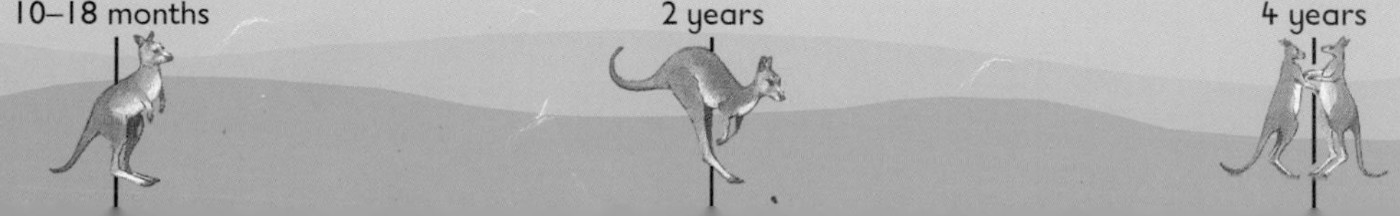

# Young Kangaroo 2 to 3 years

Now the young kangaroo is an adult. He can care for himself and he leaves his mother. He hops over the grass on his strong back legs.

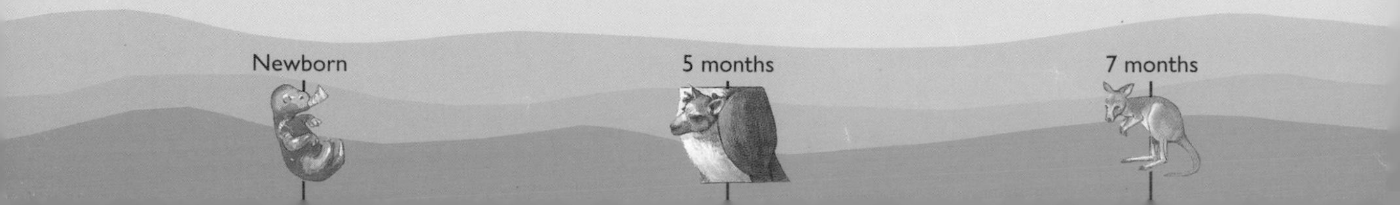

Newborn

5 months

7 months

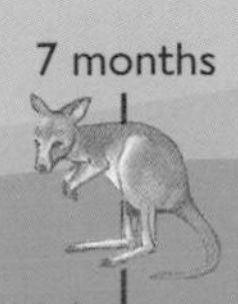

His long tail helps him to balance as he hops through the air. He joins a group of other young males.

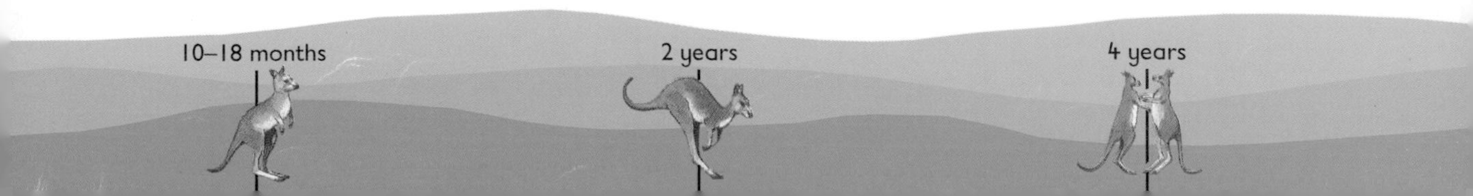

10–18 months

2 years

4 years

# Mating

## 4 years

The young kangaroo notices a female. He wants to **mate** with her, but so does another male. The two males begin to fight.

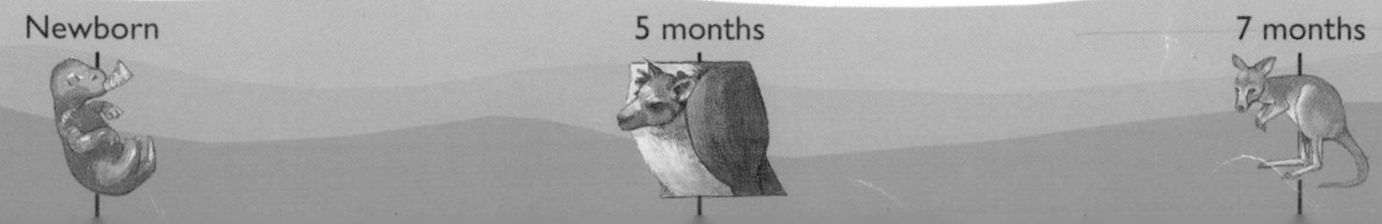

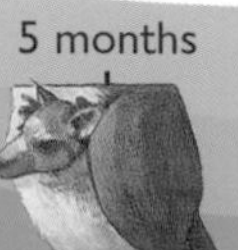

They grab each other with their front legs. The young kangaroo leans back on his tail and kicks with both feet.

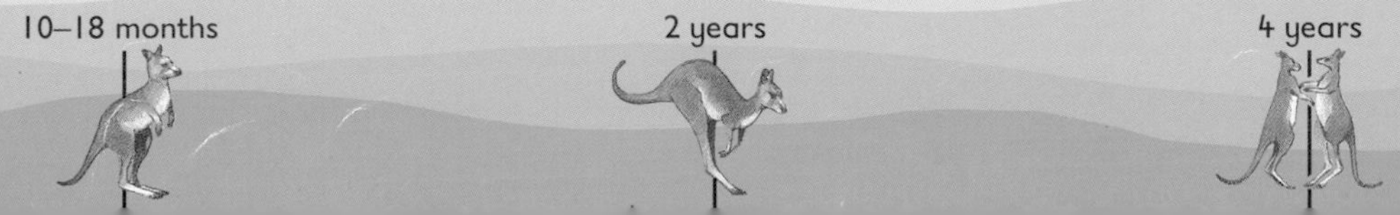

# 4 years

The female watches as the young male wins the fight. He nuzzles her and clucks gently until she is ready to **mate**.

Newborn

5 months

7 months

Forty days after mating a new **joey** will be born. It will grow inside its mother's **pouch.**

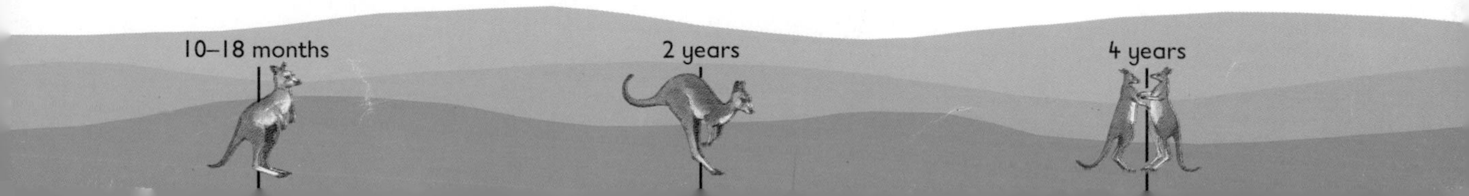

# Life in the Bush

**Dingoes** are one of the kangaroos' predators. A **pack** of dingoes can surround a kangaroo and attack it.

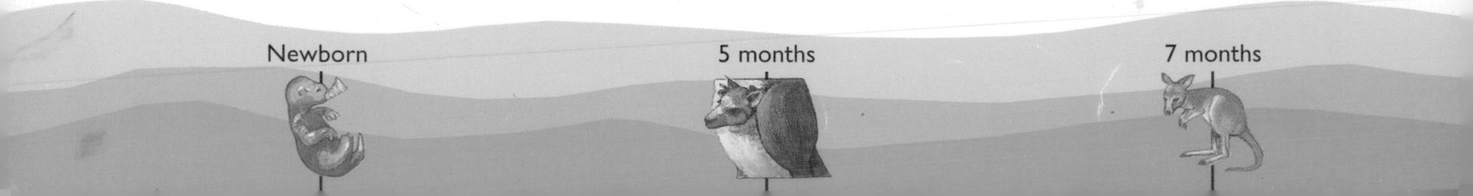

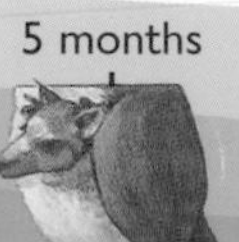


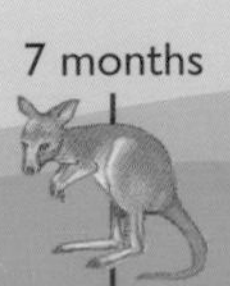

These kangaroos have smelled a dingo. They bound away, thumping the ground with their back legs as they go.

# Life in the Bush

The **dingo** isn't the kangaroo's only enemy. If a kangaroo wanders onto farmland, the farmer may shoot him.

But if the kangaroo stays in the **bush**, he may live for fifteen years grazing among the trees with the other kangaroos.

# Life Cycle

Newborn Joey

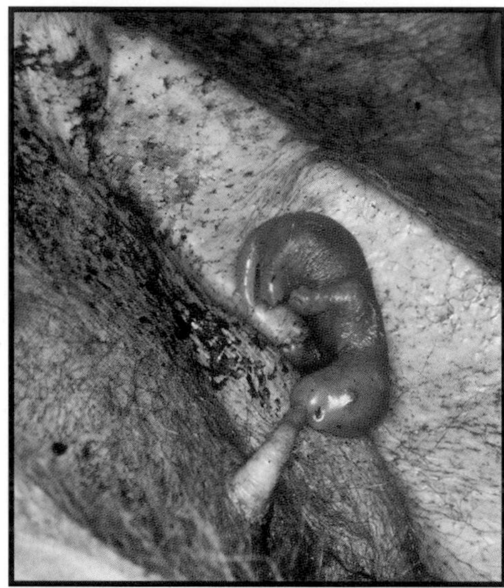

*1*

Joey

*2*

Joey

*3*

Joey

*4*

Young Kangaroo

*5*

Mating

*6*

# Fact File

A newborn **joey** is one inch long, not even as long as your little finger!

A fully grown male Grey kangaroo is as tall as a man. Some Red kangaroos grow even taller.

A kangaroo can jump 45 feet. In one bound it could jump over three cars parked end to end.

A kangaroo can move as fast as a car (up to 40 miles per hour) to escape from danger.

# Glossary

**box** playful fighting

**bush** the Australian word for open countryside

**dingo** a kind of wild dog found in Australia

**joey** a young kangaroo from the time it is born until it is old enough to look after itself

**mate** when a male and a female come together to produce babies

**pouch** a pocket of skin across a female kangaroo's stomach

**teat** a place where a baby can drink milk from its mother

# More Books to Read

Butterworth, Christine. *Kangaroos.* Chatham, NJ: Raintree Steck-Vaughn. 1990.

Lepthien, Emilie U. *Kangaroo.* Chatham, NJ: Raintree Steck-Vaughn. 1995.

Serventy, Vincent. *Kangaroo.* Chatham, NJ: Raintree Steck-Vaughn.1985.

# Index